Tomorrow We'll Draw Daisies

A Pocket Book of Pandemic Poetry

By Marie Monro

Copyright © 2021 Marie Monro

All rights reserved

No part of this book may be reproduced or used in any manner without written permission of the copyright owner.

For more information please email mariezmonro@hotmail.com

First paperback edition June 2021

Cover Art Design by Lee Hunt

ISBN 978-1-008-92205-1
Self-Published by Lulu.com

Introduction

This Pocket Book of Pandemic Poetry titled 'Tomorrow We'll Draw Daisies' is written by Marie Monro who lives on the South Coast of England.

The poetry contained within takes inspiration from experiences surrounding her during the global Covid pandemic.

With thanks to Maggie Sawkins from Tongues and Grooves for providing a few prompts to direct some creative writing opportunities during lockdown 1.0. Some earlier variations of these poems appeared on the Portsmouth Star and Garter's online publication in 2020.

Contents

Covid A-Z
April Fool
At the beginning it felt like the end
Covid Penny
Donald
Dunk-irk
Eyes on Reality
Face the Fear
Lockdown Avenues
No Ordinary Bloke
Practice What you Preach
Simple Wonder
Small Snail
Stock Pile
Taking its Toll
Tomorrow We'll Draw Daisies
Unwind
Withdrawn
A poem (ish!)
Yo! Bob

Covid A-Z

Announcement By
Covid-19 Diplomats
Expect Further Guidelines
Help Innocent Jobless
Kids Love Mum's
New Optimistic Parenting
Quit Real-life Situations
Trust UK Vaccine
Wait-on Xenodiagnostics
Yielding Zeneca

April Fool

Bojo nears the conference door
A nation waits to hear the score
He's familiarly dishevelled
His stance unduly levelled

He leans towards the microphone
An apathetic 'Stay at home'?
Financial tips on how to cope?
We listen for a glimpse of hope

The virus has clearly made him ill
Announcing a new health care bill?
He's had a change of heart he claims
He'll even stop the Brexit games

Face half covered by his flop of hair
With a swelling aristocratic air
Stumbles over an Ummm
and an arrrrhhhh, delivers the
greatest lines of his career so far

'You can all go back to work'
He says with a gleeful smirk
'You can all go back to school
Its just been an April Fool'

At the beginning it felt like the end

The first week was tough, we were grieving
We scrubbed up, cleaned up, hid behind masks
Like *The Very Hungry Caterpillar*, we ate through our food

Some acceptance arrived along with week two
Crafted, played games, cooked, baked cakes
Emptied the shelves of dried pasta, flour and yeast

In the third week, we'd all started to yawn
Netflix was booming, we all began zooming
and stayed in our pyjamas 'til late

By week four we were bored, cranky, frustrated
Body coach Joe had made us all sore
We drank wine with our brunch in the sun

We sensed a rising rebellion, approaching week five
Still resisting temptation to step outside we watched TV programmes about travel instead

Week six was beginning to wear a bit thin
Swapped slippers for shoes, turned off the news
Let the wind dry our hair, riding bikes

Covid Penny

See a Penny....

Don't pick it up

Donald

Donald Trump
did a dump
behind The White
House door

Mrs Trump
wiped it up
but Donald did
some more

Dunk-irk

1. Make a cup of tea
2. Leave used bag for next cup on spoon
3. Get biscuits for dunking
4. Theorise potential dunking times for all biscuits chosen
5. Try to draw graph to plot experiment
6. Ask kids for help as you can't remember graph plotting from school
7. Still don't get it, so get kids to draw graph instead
8. Tick off Maths home schooling task for the day
9. Conduct the dunking test experiment
10. Plot on graph with red ink
11. Findings did not match original theory
12. Return to overstocked biscuit cupboard
13. Choose more biscuits for real experiment
14. Conduct the real experiment exactly as the test experiment
15. Plot on graph with blue ink
16. Realise you'll probably need more evidence to support your theory

17. Several biscuit ends have dropped in the tea, so that probably renders the experiment parameters invalid
18. Return to line 1.

Eyes on Reality

Creases of skin, creases of eyes
Eyes that sparkle, eyes that tell lies
Lies test stories, lies test theories
Theories break banks, theories break boundaries
Boundaries cause roadblocks, boundaries cause hate
Hate can be necessary, hate can be reserved
Reserved means taken, reserved means slow revelation
Revelation leads to vulnerability, revelation leads to new horizons
Horizons will rise, horizons will change
Change is good, change is inevitable
Inevitable is hard to avoid, inevitable is hard to disregard
Disregard what is not important, disregard what I just said
Said the man with the tan, said the man pushing greed
Greed represents money, greed represents fear
Fear can be overcome, fear can be challenging

Challenging times will be faced alone, challenging times will be faced together
Together we're strong, together we're weak
Weak bones can be broken, weak bones can be cast
Cast shadows, cast doubt
Doubt nothing, doubt everything
Everything is important, everything is hurting
Hurting means we can begin to heal, hurting means we can all still feel
Feel freedom, feel reality
Reality is now. Reality is you
You, now

Face the Fear

Show

Fear

Show fear

Show no fear

Show no fear, feel more

Show no fear, feel more fearlessness

Show no fear, feel more fearlessness.
Feel the fear, do it anyway

Show no fear, feel more fearlessness.
Feel the fear, do it anyway. Face the fear,
don't stop

Lockdown Avenues

On once a Carnival lined street
Brazil bangs drums with no beat

Operatic balconies offer no immunity
Italy sings to unite their Community

The USA is brought to tears
New Zealand, shuts its doors

For all Keyworkers on the frontline
The UK cheers and claps on time

No Ordinary Bloke

He made a suggestion:
To irradicate infection
We should ingest the
disinfectant, for a joke

He's not a Doctor
but he knows
more about this than
any ordinary bloke

When asked if he'd digest it
He answered with a choke
'I'm not a Doctor
I'm just an ordinary bloke'

He seized upon the chance
to invest a billion bucks
He's as clever as the virus
He's no ordinary bloke

Practice What You Preach

You must always practice what you preach
Or your credibility will be out of reach

For example:
Dominic Cummings' lockdown breach

Simple Wonder

I find I worry more these days
I simply wonder more

Is there simply more to worry about
or have I learnt to wonder more

Here's something more to wonder
Do I simply listen more, now my life

is not like what it was before?

Small Snail

Travel slows
a small snail
with the whole world
on its back

Stock Pile

Advert
Loo roll for sale!
Forty five pence a sheet
Do not let yourself get caught short
Stock Pile

Taking its Toll

Morphing into soft-bodied drones
Socialising with the book of faces
Engaging tic-toc dances

Scrolling day after day
Draining our charge
Searching for connection

Overeating, oversleeping, overthinking
Drinking gin at silly o'clock
while the yard arm is broken

Watching World headline news
swamped by Government briefings
Waiting the day's toll to be taken

Tomorrow We'll Draw Daisies

Yesterday, we painted rainbows
Wrote the words 'Be Kind' in the arc

Today we'll go on a bear hunt
for our local, daily walk

Tomorrow we'll draw daisies
on black boards with white chalk

For now let us be quiet
Think first before we talk

Unwind

Use this time
to assess the
mental mess

Examine, sort
reflect, destress
Keep what you need

Bin the rest

Withdrawn

We were told what to do
Where to go, how to live
It was hard to follow the rules
It was not the freedom we knew

Herded into homes
Withdrawn from our lives
Swiftly collapsing upon our chests
A breathing Chapel of Rest

A Poem (ish!)

A funny-ish, hairy-ish Cornish
Pixie, behaving slightly Impish

Uttering total jibberish
Acting completely foolish

Trying to relinquish anguish
for not being cool-ish

Wants to be more Devilish
not girlish English Elfish

More Irish Leprechaun-ish
Hair all sunshine yellowish

Mopish, slightly foppish
Looking sort of hottish

Not baboonish, nor scampish
Cuter, kinda Dwarfish

Yo! Bob

Bob jogs solo on foggy moon morn. Bob lost old boot on moor

Now sock soggy, foot oddly cold. Bob stops, howls boldly to God 'Ho Bloody Ho!'

Bob slowly hops on to own front door. Oh no! Door knob drops off on to foot of no boot

Bob glows hotly – now costly job to do too. Doom 'n gloom mood looms

Cross Bob locks loo door. Plops on bog to do good sloppy poo

Bob looks for loo roll – Ooops! Bob's dog took roll for hoot

L - #0277 - 140621 - C0 - 175/108/3 - PB - DID3108037